MW01045017

Meditations For People Managers

Concise Insights For Busy Leaders

Nora A. Jones

Copyright © 2005 by Nora A. Jones.

Library of Congress Number   2005900799
ISBN: Softcover   1-4134-8531-6

All rights reserved. No part of this book may be reproduced or transmitted
in any form or by any means, electronic or mechanical, including
photocopying, recording, or by any information storage and retrieval system,
without permission in writing from the copyright owner.

This book was printed in the United States of America.

To order additional copies of this book, contact:
Xlibris Corporation
1-888-795-4274
www.Xlibris.com
Orders@Xlibris.com
23969

Dedicated to Kathryn M. Downing and David J. Oliveiri, the managers who coached me and provided the opportunities that made all the difference in my successful development of dozens and dozens of staff members. Special acknowledgement goes to the late Loretta Martello, a remarkable teacher who encouraged the development of my writing skills. And a sincere thank you to the many former employees who still seek my advice and look to me as a mentor.

Introduction

I was lucky. The boss who promoted me into management was a great mentor, in tune with the changing business world. He understood the need to break down hierarchical boundaries and to integrate related functions into self-reliant teams. Fortunately, I didn't have a lot of hierarchical baggage to unlearn. Empowering and coaching people seemed logical and felt right.

Through the 1990s I had three different assignments that involved taking groups of single-function "supervised employees," and teaching them to broaden their skill set and work as independent, problem-solving, cross-functional productive teams. Technology was changing rapidly; we were going through numerous acquisitions and mergers, downsizings, and rightsizings. Chaos was constant, and change was imperative.

In this first decade of the 21st century, I see a need to continue to expand many of the management techniques that were viewed as revolutionary only a few years ago. Developing quality staff members, gaining the respect of the entire organization, and maintaining one's authentic self in a fast-paced, spread-too-thin environment requires sharp focus on personal values and integrity. To maintain one's balance amidst this flow, a daily kernel of introspection may provide the centering that makes each day productive and positive.

Week 1

Am I tired today from too much work or too little play? What will I do this week to make next Monday better?

How am I changing the culture of this organization? Will my staff have the skills, attitude and work ethic to succeed no matter how this business changes?

We learn best when we accept our role as a beginner. I need to persuade my staff that being a beginner is a good place to start, not an awkward stage of development.

If everyone disagrees with me, perhaps I should revisit the foundation of my view.

I need to remember my own limitations. Seeking help to correct my lack of experience can only improve my credibility.

Week 2

Is my sense of urgency consistent with department results? Do my priorities align with company goals?

We are only as strong as our weakest link. What can I do today to help strengthen one of my team's weak links?

Could someone on the team accuse
me of favoritism? I will make sure
"results" are emphasized, not an
individual.

Am I holding someone back who
could be doing a portion of my work?
I'll make a conscious effort to grant
experience opportunities to those
who are deserving.

Which e-mails (good and bad) can I
save as input for someone's
performance review? Today I'll
rescue some pertinent comments
from cyberspace.

Week 3

Do my actions make sense to my
staff? What new ways can I use to tie
daily activities to our business
strategy?

In a global marketplace, distance no
longer matters. Am I operating in a
"world-wide" mindset? Am I as
open-minded as I want my staff to
be?

If too many meetings crowd my schedule, can I have someone shadow me, coaching him or her to attend a weekly meeting in my place?

Who can I surprise today with a reward or special thank you? A handwritten note could increase someone's confidence enough to allow him or her to really excel.

Have I exercised my sense of humor adequately this week? No matter how grim it looks, this is not brain surgery.

Week 4

Is there a conflict I've been avoiding
that I could resolve today? I will
actively pursue a way to work it out.

Laughter helps to stimulate the
brain. Am I surrounding myself with
stimulating people? Too much
seriousness may block true progress.

Am I allowing my disappointments to
affect my staff? My attitude will
likely be reflected in the work I get
back.

Have I increased my business
network this month? I will schedule
at least two lunches with those
outside my company who might play
an important role in some future
endeavor.

Am I utilizing all resources that can
help my department reach full
potential? Have I invited related
production groups to observe and
comment on our processes?

Week 5

Am I focused on what needs my attention the most today? I will think about company priorities before tackling what appears to be urgent to me.

Can I clarify the company goals for my staff today? A five-minute meeting might increase productivity. Understanding "why" they are doing their job can help staff members find their own ways to be more efficient.

Am I up-to-date on performance reviews? Staff trust is built on my ability to deliver on promises. If I am behind, I will communicate with those affected and set new timeframes that I will absolutely meet.

In my rush to get through the day, have I trampled on those whom I will later need to carry me forward? Perhaps I need to slow down and acknowledge that I can't do it all alone.

Is there some financial analysis one of my staff members might be able to prepare (and enjoy) that would benefit the team? One person's flair for numbers may provide welcome relief to me while stimulating and energizing him or her.

Week 6

If e-mail is taking more than 10% of my day, I need to make sure the right things are getting my attention. Are there e-mail automation tools I should leverage to my advantage?

While driving to work, I will mentally list the many positive elements of my job and take time to enjoy them throughout the day.

Does my vision of quality match the staff's vision of quality? How can I ensure that my expectations are understood and achievable?

If the company gave my team a report card today, what grade would we get? I will ask collateral departments to provide relevant feedback to ensure we are doing as well as we think we are.

Is there someone on the team pulling down the team's grade? I will speak to them today to identify ways to change this.

Week 7

Has my need to "be liked" deterred
me from dealing with a difficult
matter? I'm not getting paid to be
likeable.

Are my boss' expectations in sync
with mine? I'll touch base with my
boss today and make sure (s)he
agrees with my priorities.

Which staff member deserves a
special perk like a training
conference? Today I'll notify
someone of an opportunity that will
likely be embraced as more exciting
than a bonus paid in dollars.

Are we talking it to death?
Sometimes it is important to make a
decision and take action. If it
doesn't work out, we at least will
know more than we did while we
were debating what to do.

What money-saving idea can I
propose to senior management?
Suggestions offered before being
asked will help to demonstrate my
promotional worthiness.

Week 8

There are no dress rehearsals. Am I making the best effort to get it right the first time and learning along the way? Am I proud of my performance?

What can I do today to improve team spirit or morale? Is there a memo or e-mail from senior management that I can share to bolster team pride?

When is the last time my team heard
customer feedback? Do they know if
customers are satisfied with their
performance? Plan for a survey or
other feedback tool.

Why don't staff members come to my
office more? Are they afraid to
disturb me? Does it appear I am
never available? Without daily
dialogue, will I know what staff
members need direction on?

Am I keeping up with the technology
I expect my staff to learn? What
workshop or seminar could I take to
improve my own skills and
credibility?

Week 9

Today I will avoid sending e-mail when a face-to-face meeting or phone call might build better camaraderie and avoid misunderstandings. Personal relationships are always stronger than cyber-communications.

What team activity can we plan to build a stronger alliance? A pizza lunch or group outing might help strengthen bonds that have weakened during a production crisis.

Does my website reflect the most current department vision and org chart? I will make sure it is updated this week.

Am I depleting my emotional reserves by worrying about what may come to pass? If I focus my energy on the present, I will get more done.

Not all movement is forward. Am I rushing in the right direction today?

Week 10

What could I do today to help bridge a communication gap between two groups or individuals? As a leader, I need to be on daily patrol for obstacles that may reduce productivity.

Is there an unpleasant conversation that has been put off for too long? I will stop procrastinating so it doesn't use up my energy any longer.

What paperwork could I delegate to someone else in the group to free up my time for more strategic matters?

If I'm not improving myself, chances are those around me aren't gaining much either. I need to remember that I am an architect of human possibilities. What am I building?

Do I know the root cause of day-to-day fires that break out? Today I will implement some fire prevention tactics to ease tomorrow's load.

Week 11

Have I given my staff the right
incentives to reach the results we
need? Today I'll ask one person what
motivates him/her.

Does my staff see me as motivated or
worn out? Tonight I will go home or
go to the gym to refresh myself into a
better role model.

Are there obstacles keeping me from
enjoying my job? To what extent are
they within my control?

What accomplishments can we
celebrate to infuse energy into a
project that is languishing? Make
sure the journey has its rewards, too.

Does my team have all the
information they need to be
successful? Today I will see what I
can do to fill the gaps.

Week 12

Professional sports teams have strength and conditioning coaches. To ensure my team's top performance, are there resource or equipment issues I could address today?

Is the person in the mirror the leader I aspire to be? If not, what do I need to do today to improve my image?

What business book or magazine
have I read this month? If I'm not
staying current, I could lose my
management edge. What can I do to
be sharper by next Monday?

What have I been doing to
understand the competition? Have
we grown comfortable and
complacent? I will make sure the
staff and I keep up-to-date.

If I have suggestions for improving
other departments, have I shared
those ideas in a positive way for the
good of the company?

Week 13

How well do I understand my customers' needs? Am I supplying what they need or what I *assume* they need? Today I'll spend some time talking to a customer.

Am I hiring clones of myself? If they are all just like me, they'll make the same mistakes as me and fail "to help the boss look better."

Was a colleague's suggestion taken in the spirit of improvement of the big picture? Or was I defensive and territorial? Playing defense may prevent the other team from scoring but won't necessarily win points for my team.

Is my personal exhaustion leaking through to the staff? I should take a day off to re-energize before I contaminate the team.

What yardstick am I using to measure success? Is it the right one?

Week 14

Urgency is a point of view. Just as I observe my staff occasionally rushes off in a strange direction, am I sure I am on the right track today? Did some unexpected phone call send me off course?

If I am going to effectively lead by example, I must be certain my body language doesn't negate my words.

What loose ends have been dragging
too long? Today I will bring closure
to something that has been on my to
do list for more than 10 days.

Am I meeting or communicating
enough with a key department that
relies on my group? Today I will
arrange for a check-point meeting to
ensure collaboration.

Do my boss and I agree on realistic
target dates for certain projects?
This week I'll review what's realistic
against the planned schedule and
discuss any disparity.

Week 15

If I were in a different department, what would I want to know about this group? What can I do to ensure that others have that information?

What system of checks and balances will help ensure consistent results from project to project? Can that become the responsibility of someone on the team who enjoys metrics?

If I am feeling that my peers are
getting more opportunities and
promotions, perhaps I need to learn
from their strengths rather than
resent their progress.

Does my sense of urgency erode staff
enthusiasm or impair product
quality? Do I have a good reason to
be in that big of a hurry—
jeopardizing overall performance?

What was special about my mentors?
Am I able to duplicate those
characteristics so others will learn
from me?

Week 16

Am I being persistent or a
workaholic? I'll do better in the long
run to recognize the difference.

Powerlessness is a state of mind.
What state am I in this week? If I'm
feeling like a victim, I'd better find a
new location—physically, mentally
or emotionally.

What are the action verbs that make
a resume stand out? Do those verbs
describe my actions on a regular
basis?

Is the climate I have created
challenging or impossible? The staff
will be more enthused over a series
of short-term successes that will get
us all to the same finish line than a
giant leap that may seem like
suicide.

In my attempt to shelter my staff
from harm, am I withholding
important information when they
might have solutions to the problems
I am shielding from their view?

Week 17

What special words of praise will give a good employee the confidence to become a "star" employee?

Am I waiting for permission when I should be implementing? I can always ask forgiveness if it goes wrong.

Is the energy level of my team where it needs to be? What positive fuel will provide the impetus to get to the finish line?

Are the negative attitudes I'm seeing somehow a reflection of my expectations? Do I have doubts that are bleeding through? I need to stop the bleeding.

Does my department have all the tools it needs to be productive? This week I will ask my staff for advice on equipment, personnel, or other resource needs.

Week 18

If I appear worried, my staff will multiply that mood into a storm cloud of rumors and uncertainty. What can I do to keep those clouds from taking shape and washing away productivity?

What can I do to inspire at least one team member today? I will find five minutes to connect with someone who needs a personal boost.

Happiness begets creativity. Have I planted the right seeds and watered them with enthusiasm? Or are the team's ideas being trampled into the dirt before they sprout?

What stress relief can I provide to my team? Sometimes just explaining the budget, or a potential reorganization can bring clarity to what appears to be endless pressure.

What unreasonable expectation is blocking my view of the light at the end of the tunnel? Is the same blockage hindering team productivity?

Week 19

If I'm not passionate about my goals,
how will my staff learn to be
passionate about their goals? Do
they see me as engaged or obsessed?
My example needs to be the right
example.

To win employee trust, I must listen
to their ideas. Have I been taking
enough time to listen?

Does my staff get meaningful customer feedback to help them improve? This week I'll make sure they are privy to customer comments in one form or another.

Does my department have the skills to identify and solve problems? If not, what training and assignments am I giving them to develop those skills?

Is there a bad apple affecting the whole group? This week I will do something to counteract or reverse the impact.

Week 20

Do I fully understand the company
mission statement? When is the last
time I explained to my staff how their
goals relate to the company mission?

Is my computer replacing face-to-
face conversations? This week I will
make sure I have an extra 10
minutes of personal contact each
day by substituting a face-to-face for
an e-mail.

Do I harbor a negative perception of
a person or department? Today I will
take steps to overcome this
impression by getting more facts.

Does my competitive spirit
sometimes override the true need for
win-win solutions? This week I'll ask
myself this question in key meetings
and discussions.

Today I will list five core
competencies of my department and
I will find a creative way to publicly
recognize the team for its talent.

Week 21

Has my sense of humor gone
underground during this week's
latest crisis? If I lighten up, so will
my staff.

Do I accept the things I cannot
change or drive others crazy trying
to control things beyond my control?
Today I will consciously note what's
beyond my control and let go.

It takes a lot of courage to implement change, but it takes a lot of energy to resist it. At the end of the day, where do I want to be?

I get paid to influence others. Am I earning that portion of my paycheck by providing the best influence possible?

Today I will concentrate on the road ahead and forget the bumps in yesterday's road. Too much time spent looking backwards causes mishaps.

Week 22

Denial is a lose-lose proposition. I will admit my shortcomings or mistakes and move forward from here.

Am I being defensive? What is the underlying weakness that needs attention? If I am trying to cover for some shortcoming, I will find a mentor or training program that will help me strengthen those areas.

Does my staff know what motivates
me? If I share my motives, maybe
someone else will catch the same
excitement.

Do I understand my industry's
trends? What articles or reports will
enlighten me? I need to be prepared
to explain the trends to my staff.

Is this week's crisis a reflection of a
blind spot in my planning? I will try
harder to take the long and broad
view as I look ahead.

Week 23

Is using the same approach repeatedly failing to spark new results? What can I change in the process to improve the outcome?

Today I will strive to get yesterday's dirt out from under the carpet so I don't have to worry about it ever again.

How can I inject some new energy into my team? As a people manager, I need to stimulate, motivate, and energize the troops. What's on this week's schedule that can be leveraged to invigorate my team?

When was the last time I told my top staff member how much I appreciate his/her work? If it wasn't this week, it's been too long.

This week I will make a point of communicating the company's performance objectives for this year—to remind and reinforce how individual contributions drive results.

Week 24

Is my need for a vacation dragging down the team? The team will mirror what they see in my face.

If surveyed today, would my staff agree that they are empowered to handle their day-to-day problems? If not, what can I do to symbolically transition the power they feel they lack?

Is my staff hearing disquieting rumors? I need to apologize if I let the grapevine get ahead of me and implement safeguards to prevent it from happening in the future.

Does my department understand the business reasons behind meeting our deadlines? Perhaps I need to relay the scenario where the competition beats us.

What can I delegate today that may help someone add credentials to his or her resume? Building staff resumes helps me to build my resume.

Week 25

Self-control often brings more respect than IQ. Does my behavior reflect this wisdom?

Is the conflict within my team caused by mixed signals from me? I will identify the cause of the conflict. If even 10% of the cause was my unclear communication, I will apologize for my portion of the problem.

Am I hiding in my comfort zone?
Lack of risk-taking could make me
an easy target for the next round of
job cuts.

Do others view me as a dinosaur?
What am I doing to stay current with
technology and training?

Will my staff understand why their
colleague was promoted ahead of
them? I will ensure that everyone
knows what achievements earned the
promotions.

Week 26

Is my lack of confidence creating a leadership vacuum? Is my hesitation slowing down the team?

Have I prepared my staff for their future? Today I will identify seminars or resources that will ensure continued growth and development.

What is my succession plan? Have I faithfully given training opportunities to my staff? I should have at least two people who could handle my duties if I was called away on assignment.

What have I done this month to help my boss look good? A "press release" to the company newsletter can give both my boss and my staff the visibility they deserve.

Am I missing some key pieces of business background? Who could mentor me past these insecurities? Today I will set up a lunch date with someone who can help me.

Week 27

What professional or community organization might enhance my network of business acquaintances? I will inquire about membership and responsibilities.

Am I getting enough sleep to portray energy and enthusiasm at the office? My staff tends to mirror what they see.

Am I prepared for my own future?
What can I do today to anticipate
tomorrow's needs?

Do my under-performers know what
they need to do to improve? Today I
will help them set specific,
incremental performance goals.

Is my group clear on what success
factors are valued the most in our
organization? I will help them relate
those values to the merit increase
system.

Week 28

Am I empowering my employees to make decisions on their own? Is there a problem on my plate today that I could turn over to the staff?

Why am I waiting for my boss to call me? I will call my boss today to share a key success that may not be apparent.

Does my team know how proud I am
of them? What can I do today to let
them know?

Am I creating a competitive
atmosphere that generates energy
and innovation, or is the competition
dividing the group?

Am I angry with one of my peers?
Could it be due to lack of
communication? Have I assumed
something that may not be true?

Week 29

Do I convey the right focus in staff
assignments? Is my emphasis on
perfection delaying results? Is my
emphasis on results impairing
quality?

How many of my boss' duties could I
handle myself? How can I get the
training or experience I need to
assure him/her I am ready?

Does my staff know where the budget goes? I will set aside time to review basic economics to ensure everyone can relate to cost-cutting requirements in light of revenue short-fall.

What can I do to improve productivity of my poorest employee? Training, tools, or reassignment should be considered.

What can I do to improve team performance? Could a visual chart communicating accomplishments encourage stronger team commitment?

Week 30

Am I discouraging staff from taking risks? I will make sure we celebrate both successes and failures to demonstrate the importance of trying new ideas.

What am I doing to develop a solid replacement for myself? My accomplishments may be short-lived if no one understands how to carry them out after I move on.

Am I afraid to take a risk and try
something new? When is the last
time I tried something "outside the
box" without getting my boss'
permission?

Am I over-analyzing and moving too
slowly for today's business world? I
will identify what is preventing
forward movement and seek a
solution to insure that we keep pace.

What efficiency suggestion can I
make to improve company profits? If
I wait to be "asked," it might be too
late.

Week 31

How do I personally influence the productivity of the organization? This week I will consciously observe how my own actions are affecting those around me.

How can I get my subordinates to generate new ideas? Perhaps a wall chart or point system can encourage broader participation and more frequent contributions.

What can I do to make the job more rewarding for my staff? I'll arrange a visit from top brass or a photo in the company newsletter to provide deserved recognition.

What part of my job do I do best? Is it the primary reason my boss selected me for this job or have I adjusted the job to suit my strengths?

What is my next career move? Am I getting the training and experience I need to get there? If I don't have direction in my own life, am I a good leader?

Week 32

Is someone waiting for a decision from me? Today I will bring closure to an open issue that may have inadvertently slipped from front and center.

What is the biggest misperception about me? How can I change that image? Today I will commit to a new habit that will steer perceptions away from an image I am trying to shake.

Does my boss agree with my current
list of top priorities? When is the
last time I reviewed my own goals
with my boss? Perhaps it is time to
compare and synchronize.

Which reports could I live without?
Will elimination of those reports
save the company some time? Today
I will discuss these potential time-
savers with colleagues or superiors.

What are my long-range plans for
developing my subordinates? Can I
get the budget dollars I need to do
it? This week I will outline what I
need to have versus what would be
ideal.

Week 33

If schedules seem unrealistic, what have I done to change them? My staff counts on me to support their success and if I am not convinced their goals can be met, what am I doing about it?

Why don't I delegate more? If I think it takes too much time to train someone, then I will always be locked into working 12-hour days.

How long has it been since I've
given my subordinates some
individual feedback? Today I will
talk to at least two people about their
performance, good, bad, or
otherwise.

Am I in over my head? Where can I
get help? This week I will play
offense rather than defense.

Do I have all the facts to have this
conversation? Perhaps I need to
listen more and talk less.

Week 34

What areas do I micro-manage?
What will help me stop? This week I
will consciously let go of details that
are well-handled by others.

Am I poised under pressure? How
can I do better? When I see someone
struggling with pressure, what can I
learn and implement for myself?

Do I set a good example by creating
and following a meeting agenda? For
the next month, I will prepare and
follow an agenda for all meetings I
chair.

Do my direct reports have a sense of
ownership? Perhaps I meddle too
much, making them think I don't
trust them. This week I will make a
point of acknowledging the value of
their independent judgment.

Am I patient when I listen to new
ideas from staff or does my rush to
get to the next thing discourage
innovation?

Week 35

Am I still punishing someone for bygone mistakes? This week I will have a conversation or write a letter that will clear the air of stale issues.

Would all my direct reports assess my approach as fair and equitable? Today I will pretend a camera is capturing my actions and watch for deviations from even-handedness.

Today I will consider who might be unclear on their objectives and spend 10 minutes clarifying next steps. Today's 10 minutes could save weeks of rework.

I will take time to clear some clutter from my e-files or file cabinets. It may not be obstructing my focus today, but tidying up might prevent future obstacles.

Do all of my actions show my commitment to excellence? If I am sending a mixed message, I need to eliminate contradictory behaviors.

Week 36

Am I becoming complacent? Am I
tolerating inefficiencies that a new
manager would tackle the minute I
leave? Change doesn't require a new
person, only a new attitude.

Passionate belief will yield
extraordinary results. If I've lost my
passion, I should move on to an area
where my passion will drive success.

Associate with successful people.
Active listening works as well as
asking for help. I need to be
conscious of who I hang out with.

Generate enthusiasm for something.
Ten minutes of enthusiasm can
ignite an otherwise routine day.

Do I remember to tell colleagues,
family, and friends what role they
play in my success? Tell five people
how much I appreciate them.

Week 37

Courage is the ability to act despite
my fears. What have I been avoiding
and what can I do today to get
beyond that obstacle?

Does my staff view me as a help or a
hindrance? Maybe I need to stay out
of their way so they can succeed.

I'd rather have 10 minutes of
excellence than a lifetime of
mediocrity. What can I do to initiate
one noteworthy success that will
shine on my resume or the
company's record?

Have I become a generalist with
average output, or a specialist who
can do only one thing? Today I will
choose one task or skill to improve
to regain sharpness and balance.

Am I still living by my commitment
to always tell the truth? Has some
work situation infringed upon my
personal values? Today I will revisit
my standards and adjust my
behavior accordingly.

Week 38

Attitudes are contagious. What am I
spreading?

What can I do today to show support
services (building maintenance, mail
services, other) that they are
appreciated? It is always nice to
reinforce working relationships
before a crisis tests their strength.

In talking with a staff member, do I provide clear-cut instructions or objectives? Am I the reason their output falls short of department goals? Maybe I need to assign a "tutor" who communicates differently to get through to this person.

Have I compromised my own integrity to avoid a conflict? The price of an unpleasant confrontation should not bankrupt my value system.

How much I care is as important as how much I know. Would my family recognize this as my motto? Does my staff know this about me?

Week 39

Today I will revive my sense of
humor and make work fun. A good
dose of laughter can stimulate
productivity beyond expectations.

If I can't change the circumstances
perhaps I need to change my
attitude. I always have control over
my own attitude.

Delivering a compliment may be a
perfect reward for certain
achievements. Am I being stingy
with praise? This week I will dip into
the well of compliments to refresh
the energy of my team.

Empathy and active listening were
central to the bosses I liked most.
Will my staff recognize my strength
in these areas?

When is the last time I admitted to
my own mistakes? If it appears I am
afraid to admit error, how can I
expect my staff to be forthcoming
about mistakes?

Week 40

As I approach a performance problem, have I couched it in constructive terms? Will I encourage future success or has my coaching sounded more like punishment?

Body language may be telling my staff a different story than my words. I need to consciously avoid mixed signals if I want whole-hearted success.

Does my listening posture convey openness, interest, and confidence? Active listening involves the entire body, not just the ears and mind.

Do I sometimes blame others for problems and then wonder why my staff fails to take responsibility for their mistakes? It is not unusual for a working relationship to influence behaviors, so I need to be conscious of the seeds I plant.

What are my talents? Am I in the right job to allow the things I am naturally good at to shine?

Week 41

Have I confused my talents with my skills? Through education and experience I have acquired certain abilities. Skills can earn a living. Combining skills with talent creates a career.

What would I recommend to a younger version of myself? Do I openly share those pointers with my staff? There is no reason to withhold life's lessons.

Are my personal values in line with those of my colleagues? Am I expecting relationships and commitments that don't match the temperament and experience of others?

Are my meetings and e-mails concise and to the point? Without being abrupt, I need to be conscious of time constraints and provide bite-sized pieces of accurate information.

No one can push my buttons unless I let them. Today, I won't let them.

Week 42

Am I expecting too much and allowing my apparent disappointment to discourage others? Today I will start small and recognize the incremental successes.

Am I keeping the kind of records I would want from someone else? Will my successor have to reinvent the wheel? This week I will make sure I document processes and behaviors that will prevent future redundancy.

What new things have I learned
lately? If I'm not learning on a
regular basis, I am probably growing
stagnant. Stagnant is not a
description I'd want to put on my
resume.

Enthusiasm and determination are
key ingredients to success. Do I
have the right mix to compliment my
skills and talents? What can I do
this week to adjust the formula?

Am I phrasing my questions and
expectations in the most positive
way possible? Do I remember to ask,
"How can I make this work?" rather
than "Will this work?" If I convey
doubt, how will the staff react?

Week 43

To update my resume, I need to focus on how my contributions have added to the success of the business. Did I start my work day today with those buzz words (contribution, success) in mind?

Is there a community activity or effort that would strengthen the teamwork in my group? This month I will find a project that can benefit both my staff and the community.

When I hear my staff talk in negative
terms, is it because they hear me do
it? From a leadership position, my
coworkers should never hear me
badmouth a person or project.

Can I benefit from broadening my
experience? By reaching beyond my
comfort zone, I may find the solution
to a long-standing issue in a place I
never looked before.

Do I utilize the best attributes of
both electronic and paper files? If it
takes me more than a few minutes to
find something, what am I doing to
improve the system?

Week 44

Does my staff know that I am
concerned about their professional
growth? Perhaps a wall chart
portraying training commitments will
help communicate this as a priority.

If something has rocked my
optimism or self-confidence, what do
I need to do to regain solid footing?
This week I will reach out for
assistance to ensure this uncertainty
is short-lived.

Does my staff understand how the
actions of senior management relate
to the company goals? Can I arrange
for more inter-level communication
to promote consistency from the
bottom up?

Sometimes we have to forget what
worked in the past. Sometimes we
have to forget what failed in the past.
If I approach problems with an open
mind, solutions may be closer than
they appear.

Do my team members know the
difference between strategy and
tactics? This week I will make a
point of communicating how their
day-to-day efforts (tactics)
contribute to the company's overall
business plan (strategy).

Week 45

Do I provide enough opportunities
for my staff to stay current with
technology? If I hold them back,
they will hold me back.

Is my perfectionism ruining morale?
Are my obsessive tendencies
causing excessive staff turnover? Is
my need for perfection moving me
further and further from my goals?

Would I be willing to invest in this company? Am I doing everything I can, as a leader, to ensure that shareholders believe in me and my team's ability?

When speaking to senior management, do I properly praise my team and key players? If I lead them to believe the success is all mine, next year's budget may be for a staff of one.

In our effort to multi-task, have we lost the ability to concentrate? Do we model chaos at a frantic pace? This week I will be conscious of my methods and ensure that interruptions and distractions don't make me inefficient.

Week 46

Is there a project that I am avoiding
due to a time commitment? Can I
break it into several more
manageable chunks and get it
started this week?

Aerobic exercise improves memory.
Is my confusion or frustration at
work related to my physical
inactivity? I will make time for
exercise and see if my thinking
clears.

Am I viewing my problems as opportunities to learn something new? If not, I should make some adjustments in my attitude to revive my enthusiasm for learning.

Is my own system of information management as good as I demand from my staff? What electronic and hard copy files will make me more efficient?

Does my staff know what risks I have taken in my career? Am I the role model they need to succeed? If it looks too easy, they may not realize the level of effort necessary to succeed in a leadership role.

Week 47

Do I select the best words for getting my point across? Do I elicit negative reactions by inadvertently talking down to staff members or confusing my listeners with complex words and concepts? This week I will practice using concise, upbeat terms.

Do I sometimes use industry jargon to show off my intelligence? Chances are my audience will lose interest or view me as narrow-minded and inconsiderate. I'll keep my audience in mind, and use appropriate terminology.

Do I use expressions or cliches that make me sound colloquial or snobbish? Neither my superiors nor direct reports want to be inundated with my quirky sayings, so I need to use them sparingly.

Communication is much more than a good vocabulary, but a good vocabulary can improve communications. What can I learn from someone I find easy to listen to and understand?

Do I share knowledge openly with others? What can I do to ensure that my colleagues and coworkers view me as a valuable and selfless resource?

Week 48

When in doubt, I need to consider the direction my instincts would take. Doing something by the book doesn't always make it right. Sometimes the book is written for a different set of facts.

If my staff is afraid to ask for help, there is a good chance they will be stuck as underachievers. How can I make sure they are comfortable asking for the instruction and tools they need?

In the hiring process, what
impressed me about one or two
resumes? Can I incorporate those
concepts into my resume?

Do I know what motivates my boss?
Would it be helpful to have that
knowledge? This week I will make a
point to ferret that information from
our conversations.

In my network of associates, who can
best help me with my current
dilemma? Today I will contact him/
her to bounce my ideas off of a
valued resource, adding clarity to
my decision-making process and
conveying a compliment to their
expertise.

Week 49

When is the last time I attended a
trade show or professional
conference? Do I know what the
latest trends and buzz words are?
Perhaps I need to refresh my
exposure to life beyond the office.

In writing performance reviews, am I
careful to consider the entire review
period and not just a recent project
or incident? How would I feel if my
boss focused on something that took
only a small percentage of my year?

When did I last take a staff member to a meeting with me to get their input on a new project or old problem? Is that individual competent to sit in for me? That will boost their morale and free up my schedule.

Are my lists helping me to accomplish the right priorities? At the end of the day, did I fall short of my listed expectations? Is it my list or my expectations that need to be adjusted?

Anger does not change minds. Do I sometimes forget this simple fact when dealing with those who disagree with me?

Week 50

What terms might my boss use to
describe me? Are they the same
terms I would use? What do I need to
do to reconcile the two lists?

Do I delegate decision-making or
only tasks? I can only build trust
and respect by delegating both.

Is my staff afraid to admit to their mistakes because of past repercussions? How can I teach them that covering up mistakes or placing blame elsewhere only compounds the problem?

Do I admit my own mistakes without a defensive attitude? This is another area where I need to lead by example.

Does my staff understand that persistence is more powerful than genius? All the brains in the world won't pay the bills unless some action is taken on great ideas.

Epilogue

Don't just think about it, do it.

BVG